WHEN WE BECOME
WEAVERS

Queer Female Poets on the Midwestern Experience

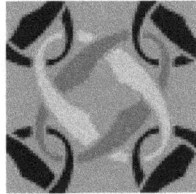

WHEN WE BECOME
WEAVERS
Queer Female Poets on the Midwestern Experience

KATE LYNN HIBBARD
Editor

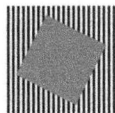

SQUARES & REBELS
Minneapolis, Minnesota

ACKNOWLEDGMENTS

The editor wishes to thank the following people:

- Raymond Luczak for his inspiration to create this anthology and for kindly and expertly guiding me through the process of making it a reality.
- The contributors for their inspiration, passion, and vision.
- Our readers for their faith in poetry.
- My partner Jan for her keen eye and for making me laugh nearly every day for the past 14 years.

COPYRIGHT

Handtype Press, LLC
PO Box 3941
Minneapolis, MN 55403-0941
squaresandrebels@gmail.com

Squares & Rebels, an imprint of Handtype Press, focuses on the LGBT experience in poetry, fiction, and creative nonfiction, preferably with a Midwestern connection. [squaresandrebels.com]

Printed in the United States of America.

ISBN: 978-0-9798816-6-4
Library of Congress Control Number: 2012943699

A First Squares & Rebels Edition

ADRIENNE RICH
6 MAY 1939 – 27 MARCH 2012
IN MEMORIAM

Learning to Weave

by Kate Lynn Hibbard

By dedicating this volume to the memory of Adrienne Rich, I have given myself an impossible task. How grandiose it feels to set this humble anthology against the vast, brilliant, necessary body of her work. And yet, I have to try. As a poet, feminist, and lesbian (not necessarily in that order), it is inconceivable for me, and for many other lesbian poets, to imagine being any one of those things without her.

At the beginning of this project, when Raymond Luczak proposed that each of us edit "companion" anthologies of gay and lesbian poets of the Midwest, I was at once excited by the possibilities but also unsure of where to draw the boundaries. What does it mean to be from the Midwest? And for that matter, what does it mean to be lesbian?

In "Compulsory Heterosexuality and Lesbian Existence," an essay from her 1986 book *Blood, Bread, and Poetry*, Rich suggests that lesbian existence is "both the fact of the historical presence of lesbians and our continuing creation of the meaning of that existence." She posits that all women exist on a lesbian continuum, a "range—through each woman's life and throughout history—of woman-identified experiences, not simply the fact that a woman has had or consciously desired genital sexual experience with another woman."

Since she wrote those words, our cultural understanding of the varieties of experience along the sex, gender, and identity continuums has virtually exploded. It soon became apparent to me that "lesbian" was too narrow a definition for the poetry of our community. Although "queer" and "female" are also loaded words that mean different things to different people at different times, they seem better suited to serve as an umbrella term for the experiences of the writers in this volume.

What, besides female queer identity, do the writers in this book have in common? The short answer: abuse, beauty, grit, wit, histories (not necessarily in that order). And what led me to choose their poems?

From Rich's biography in *The Encyclopedia of American Poetry*: "To a significant extent, all poets are concerned with transformation. The very making of a poem involves a transformation from perceived reality or experience into a verbal utterance shaped by the poet's imagination and craft. For Adrienne Rich, however, transformation goes beyond the act of writing;

FOREWORD

it extends to the culture at large through the poem's ability to challenge given assumptions and offer new visions."

I have chosen the poems in this volume with an eye toward how the poets employ craft to shape their experience, yes. But it is also equally important to me that these poems embody a mantra from the earlier women's movement that still resonates with a righteous truth: the personal is political. We do not have experiences of racism, sexism, classism, and homophobia in a vaccuum. We owe it to ourselves as poets and to the world as citizens to use our art to "challenge given assumptions and offer new visions." Carla Christopher tells us there is "Always a Survivor in the Room." Why must that still be true in 2012? The strands of poverty and drug abuse caught in Jes Braun's "Family Tree" and the harsh realities retold in Natalie Byers's "Poor White Girls" and Crystal Boson's "the metaphysics of nigger hating"—though William Carlos Williams famously said that "it is difficult to get the news from poems," it's not so hard to find it here.

Yes, these writers are survivors in many senses of that word. They endure with the grit of C. Beth Loofe speaking truth to power in "aiming at the earth," in Jennifer-River Eller's defiant "Trans* Love." They survive with the ache of childhood in Christine Stark's excerpt from her novel *Nickels: Tales of Dissociation*, caught here in the voice of a ten-year-old character. In "Mama Calls Me Anna," Andrea Jenkins survives with the strength of her mother's love, while Laura Madeline Wiseman's "The Matriarch" gives us another vision of how maternal love manifests.

A number of these writers map histories beyond the personal. Ching-In Chen's "Heritage" includes language from Victor Jew's *'Chinese Demons': the Violent Articulation of Chinese Otherness and Interracial Sexuality in the U.S. Midwest, 1885-1889*. Valerie Wetlaufer's "Call & Response" tells the story of two queer women who lived as man and wife in Wisconsin in the 1890s. Morgan Grayce Willow's "North Door" is one of several poems told from the point of view of a barn as witness to events both personal and historical.

But what makes this queer female experience Midwestern? In her submission letter, Sheila Packa writes: "It's an interesting question—what does it mean to be LBTQ and living in the Midwest? I don't know if it's because of being lesbian, but it seems I feminize and eroticize the landscape. Female energy is very powerful. It is both erotic and spiritual and transcends all boundaries." That energy abounds in her poem "Fox, No Longer Hidden," and is echoed by many other poets in this volume.

But the Midwest is not only the site of the pastoral—and in fact, the pastoral is not always such a peaceful condition, as witnessed in Jane

Eastwood's "Misericord" and Julie Gard's "Ticks." The Midwest is home to Chicago, after all, the third largest city in the U.S., and Jessica Verse Gabrielle represents hip-hop energy via "Lesbian Thoughts," while Rebecca Weaver takes us to an urban dance club in "Burn Scene."

When weaving together the poems into a whole, I thought long and hard about the title. How best to represent both the variety and the unity of these writers? No anthology can tell the whole story or fully represent the experience of its writers, of course. This volume is merely a snapshot, a moment captured in time. Once again, I turn to Adrienne Rich to help me explain my thinking. In her essay "Women and Honor: Some Notes on Lying," she deconstructs, long before that term was in vogue, the idea of "truth":

> There is no "the truth," "a truth"—truth is not one thing, or even a system. It is an increasing complexity. The pattern of the carpet is a surface. When we look closely, or when we become weavers, we learn of the tiny multiple threads unseen in the overall pattern, the knots on the underside of the carpet.

There it was. I had my permission to finish the anthology, and my title to best represent the Midwest queer female experience herein. I hope you enjoy exploring these multiple threads.

Black Ice

I go back to the girl
her blades on black ice

crossing visible cracks
fracture fused by zero

on the December lake
over fish in descending currents

silver and precise
to turn and reverse

with her fingers burned by cold
and face red-cheeked

intoxicated with chance
carving the surface of her life

with hardly a glance
in wide circles and backward

keeping weight off the landing
racing from shore

to lift when she leaped
release the pain in her feet

almost blue. Exertion or
fate.

Drowning was very near the place
we could break through.

SHEILA PACKA

Fox, No Longer Hidden

in winter, a fox crossed the path I took —
marked the slope
with cautious feet
made a hurried leap
from dark spruce
into the undergrowth of white lace
into silent snow
through grass kneeling under the weight

upon the clouds of cold
her tail floats

three months later — it was morning —
when I turned, she was waiting
at the bottom of the hill
taking the sunlight into her coat
she was a red clay halo
burnishing the agates with her heat
pouring copper into the puddle
gone before I could reach that place

now she follows me everywhere
even to this page
I see among the vowels
marked in darker ink
traces of her meandering —
hear under the birdsong her soft growls

my lovely hunter
her tail is my rudder

Red Clover

If you ask me who I am
I will tell you
I'm the daughter of red clover
blooming long in the field.

Girls braid me into their hair
wear me like jewels.
Lovers rake me
with careless fingers.

I am the daughter of red clover
from the sea of green. I am fed
by other leaves, grow wild,
am tickled by bees.

I've gone to seed
and come back, been trampled
but revive, a daughter of red clover—
one among many, a source of honey.

SHEILA PACKA

Refuge

for Meridel LeSueuer

below the canopy I am in my bed
overtaken by shadow

the crowns of the oaks carried the wind
to the pines and the pines now lean with age
and come down

who can bear the weight?

I hear the leaves of aspen
through the open window
wheels spinning on their axles

tiny insects ascending in bars of light

the surface of the lake glints like silver-plate
underneath are stones
broken by ice or split by root
they crack and thud and grind

in the distance, a strong woman singing

I pull my knees up and make mountains
I make valleys and prairie

The Cost

While the maple leaves have flamed
and gone out
the leaves of the small cherry
cling and tremble.

I write myself on these.
I've shed so many things
in my life. I write myself
in the river, in the wind.

Water drips from the eaves
of my tiny house
to the shining blue stones below.
Everything must go.

CARLA CHRISTOPHER

May My Daughter Be Erotic

My Mama rocks notes like an orchestra
symphonic seduction
tumbling out over rolling hill lips
pooling between the
curving valleys that are her hips
I slid out on a rainbow
awash with salty juices that
made me a mermaid
A natural born fisher
of women
of men
There is nothing better
than the legacy of voodoo goddess rising
Grandmother to Mother and
Mother to Daughter
My sweet young thing
may the apple be rich
and not far from the tree
the nectar, a cooling slide
between the unfurling buds of your breasts

These Breasts of Mine

Thank you ancestors for these breasts
that have earned me free coffee
and a place in line closer to the ticket window
than my running late rights
should have granted me
That make art from a V neck
and rescue little black dresses
from visual obscurity
Thank you mother
for these breasts
that forced me to arch my back
and toss up my chin
to counter balance their weight
That gave me a strut walk
head high and back straight
and made men hold open doors
to dirty looks from their women
only my breasts don't believe in competition
We can out do all these men together
Thank you creator
for breasts that play well with the curves
of my striding length legs and capable shoulders
I am a landscape in pairs
My symmetry and order a testament
to your perfect plan demanding I acknowledge
these breasts are outstanding

CARLA CHRISTOPHER

Always a Survivor in the Room

I just want you to know
it wasn't your fault
You didn't lead him on
You didn't ask for it
with the flirty dips of your unguarded movement

I say this because
there is always a survivor in the room

It wasn't because you let yourself be alone
in the company of someone not to be trusted
and it wasn't because you had a drink
too strong for your untested constitution
It wasn't the shirt
the skirt
the arch in your high-stepping foot
or the come hither crook of your pretty fingers

I share this because
there is always a survivor in the room

It wasn't the seduction of darkness
It wasn't the strength of his need
He didn't get carried away
by the mindless actions of his seed
It's not because you were cold
It's not because he had to teach you
instruct you, revenge upon you
right upon your body all the wrongs
of his emasculated brothers
just seeking a softer bed
to lay their suffering upon

I speak this truth to you
because there is always a survivor in the room

She doesn't have to stand
She doesn't have to speak
She continues to put one foot in front of the other
and walk toward the day justice
is meted out in this world or the next
and her stride leaves a pathway
of loveliness blooming in her invisible footsteps
Sister, in case you haven't heard this yet today
You are beautiful
You are deserving of love
and I say this because

there is always
a survivor
in the room

LAURA MADELINE WISEMAN

Adolescence

You have all seen this: the girl,
breasts hard and sore as fists

and a body capable of lifting
itself between the metal bars

on the playground. Watch her
lose it: the bravado, the muscle

in her arms, and the wide stance
as her hat and glasses are snatched off.

She blinks, half-blind.
She holds herself captive there,

at this moment of change
and tries to fix on who did it.

It could be anyone, a bully,
a stranger, a parent, or herself.

(Aren't they all the same?) To her,
we murmur of the loss of such things

as innocence. She knows nothing
of perspective, of who she was—

legs that flew across the ground,
a mouth toughened with sass

and laughter—a memory that jars
with who she's becoming.

LAURA MADELINE WISEMAN

Mating Call

As you wait for the bus, mid-March, you hear
from a red truck a voice that trumpets,
I just had sex! and see a cab full of college boys.

The business world in open wool coats
strides the sidewalks and crosswalks
in a concussion of shiny boots and heels.

Teenagers in slim, colorful sweaters
tip their heads together in whispers
that erupt in infectious giggles.

In every thatch of winter grass, robins,
sparrows, and finches warble their song
as the sun caresses daffodils up.

Joyous, raucous children we all are
in spring, unstopping our tongues
to call out these barbaric yawps.

Boarding the bus for home, you can't help
but remember, that first thrill so high
in your throat, you too could've shouted

from an open window speeding along
to strangers who may have forgotten.
Listen, that young voice trills, *how good!*

LAURA MADELINE WISEMAN

Prayer

It is the girl with a tear penned
in black ink, black hair lifting

as she walks against the hallway's flow
who will love me, red flannel unbuttoned,

grunge band tee-shirt, black jeans, black
sneakers, fingers bitten to the quick,

the way she'll sing "Sober," candles
guttering, incense burning. I open

her folded notes, her words,
blood-stained. Yes: this is high school

romance, hormones, under our parents'
noses, but bless them, their alcoholic

nights, their days high, forgive them
for fucking up, for letting us

couple like school girls on her floor,
their couch, Eddie Vedder crooning his song.

Purity

I.

My student extends her hand with the ring,
an intricate web of crosses, hearts
within larger hearts, like a Celtic knot,

cast in silver. On the other she twists
the engagement, babbles over the proposal,
other rings she swore on and took off.

As teacher, I ask for the poem, aware
of her ruddy face, her damp eyes,
the rushed cadency of questions

on form, the assignment, my expectations.
I admit, I also study the ring—a loose fit
on her dry, flushed, and young hands.

I've heard of these rings, but never seen one,
this symbol that means virgin and pure,
a bright badge, like a scarlet letter in reverse.

II.

At seventeen, a girl knelt between my thighs
during an overnight, her dark bedding
on the floor, the blinds rolled together,

the ringing phone lifted, then settled on its hook,
the thrum of music. I didn't know anything
but her warm breath on my skin, her fingers inside

me, the flicker of her tongue, the fiery force of it.
The hot coal of first love glows red,
even now, as I breathe into that memory.

There weren't rings then, nor are there now
for some promises. I think of the soft weight
of her hips, the smudged oval of her nipples,

of what we made that weekend night,
and made again and again on her couch, her bed,
my bed, how bright it was in all that dark,

how we had to make it to know we were real, alive,
how the spark between us was so pure.
It lit up the wide world around us.

Seventeen

Down the block, three teens trumpeting
into the quiet of a late Friday afternoon,
only finches and a lone car to answer them
—school's out, the first day it feels like spring—
with jackets open, backpacks loose on their shoulders,
heads tipped back, prickly throats exposed,
and calling out hormonal nonsense—*Whoa!*

You track their sounds up the hill,
across the street, half wishing them silent,
and half nostalgic for rule breaking, for boys
who grabbed you hard at the waist, for girls
who pressed against you to smell your skin,
for long walks to nowhere, bullshitting.

When they're finally gone, it's really you
disappearing into some apartment, parents leaving
for the nightshift and you're ready to try anything,
the long neck of Black Velvet, his lips, hers.

LAURA MADELINE WISEMAN

The Matriarch

Of course we knew about the parties, the smoke
of bad girl, the tight jeans of the twenties,

dark eyes, full-breasts, hips narrow as a boy's. Yes,
she was a sex kitten—her coquettish laugh pealed

with the sugar of strawberry daiquiris, fine hands,
high cheek bones, big hair, curled and scented.

Of course she gave head, tried any man once,
passed the pipe, took it when offered, inhaled,

talked shit, gave shit, put up with shit, with people
shitting on her. Of course she got pregnant,

aborted two, gave birth to three, knowing
the fun was elsewhere and to get there,

starving, walking for miles to nowhere,
sweeping on blush, mascara, and shadows.

What we never understood, what we dismissed
with our, *That's the way mom is,* was the way

she hooked up the phone to a tape deck to record
incoming and outgoing calls, deadlocking her room,

searching our bedrooms and diaries, baiting us
with accusations of fucking, whose dick we sucked,

where we really were. What we understood
was the perfume dabbed at the throat, the husky voice,

our hands reaching to touch another's warmth,
the low neckline, the easy to undo buttons, the desire.

What we were called: *Whores, just like your mother.*

Seasoning

Air above the corn field
is still, hangs heavy
with summer moisture,
rests against tassels
and in cottonwoods bordering the field
to the west and south.
Long twilight is earth's
one content moment in the day.
The sun's rays, interrupted
by a frame the leaves make,
edge time for us.
We could almost believe
it will do as we ask,
stand still for us. But just then
one, and another, then several, soon
an extravagance of fireflies blink,
each one lasting just long enough
for the eye to find
where it no longer is,
long enough to flavor the night
with light.

MORGAN GRAYCE WILLOW

Fiddlesticks

my grandmother exclaims
when the skillet slips
from her soapy hands
and clatters to the kitchen floor.
I pick it up
and hand it back to her
to be washed all over again,
though its dents
have already been scoured
free of scorch or any specks
from the pot's portion of goulash.

Uncle Billy was a fiddler.
He traveled by surrey
or sleigh, she says,
as many as thirty miles
to play a barn dance
or wedding, back the next day
if summer, in time for haying.
The fiddle in winter
beneath the horsehide rug,
cradled him and Aunt Rose.

My grandmother's fine blue veins
were strung like cat gut
over her temple
and at her wrist,
especially in the morning,
six o'clock sharp,
when her right hand plunged
the syringe into a pinch of her thigh
to deliver its vial of insulin.

At holiday dinners,
after meat and potatoes,
Grandma would cut herself a two-inch square
of chocolate cake,
precise and deliberate as a minor scale.
I'd lose track of crop talk,
of her litanies of marrying cousins
and babies born. I prepared instead
for the catch should she slide
to the dining room floor.

MORGAN GRAYCE WILLOW

North Door

I told the child
not to sit so close
to the edge, pudgy legs,
and dimpled knees,
at first just swinging
from my haymow door.
The north door, built
low for tossing hay
to cows below,
out finally in spring
air, the pastures not
green enough
to feed them.
She didn't
understand me.
Pigeons fussed
about their nests
in my cupola. They
were no help.

She watched swallows
packing mud, her black eyes
tracing blue-brown flash, those tails
twittering a webwork
of light.
I heard a voice
from inside: "Get over here,
outta' that door." I took it
to be a brother calling,
as a parent might have done,
though he was both
too young, and
    too late.

Sometimes
butterflies come
to that height early
in the year. Yellow
or white ones, airing
sticky wings, trying flight
for a first or second
time. Can't blame
the butterfly, girl's hand,
plump and reaching,
too far, and just
far enough
for earth to take
  over.

        The brother
found her. Dog ran
barking, then growling
to the gate, pressed itself
between posts, pawing ground
to get to its favorite charge,
brother screaming
from the door above.
        Worse, the farmer,
wrench still in hand, unbuckled
boot slipping
to the gate.

The dog got there
first. Sniffed, nudged her,
then tasted blood
where three-year-old head
hit corner of feed trough.
        The dog did all
that child's whimpering,
her eyes
mercifully closed
by the time the father
arrived.

MORGAN GRAYCE WILLOW

H-O-R-S-E

The big boys hung a hoop
on a crossbeam in the hayloft,
beside the feed chute.
Any season, hot or cold,
sneakers pounded the floor,
dodging loose boards, jumping holes.
On the coldest days,
the ball barely bounced,
its air echoing like sonar from the deep.
Didn't matter. Hoop and tattered net.
Backboard made of plywood.
Fading paint a makeshift foul line.
Studs marked the out-of-bounds.
They all came, including neighbor boys,
and the one girl who tagged behind her brothers,
them spelling out H-O-R-S-E
two, even three times
before she got to O.

Until she grew into it,
year after year, getting taller and better.
They'd change her handicap,
move her farther from the hoop.
She quickened her dodge,
her drop step, her dribble.
She slid in and out,
pivoting around them,
backing them up the lane.
Keen on the angles
from backboard to hoop,
she matched their dunks
with bank shots, with lay-ups.
Unshakable on defense,
her arms wild windmills.
And she could elevate
off that uneven floor,

sudden as a cat, unpredictable.
She kept winning more games
until they claimed she cheated
and marched down that ladder,
refusing to play, the whole lot of them,
except one brother who stayed,
drilled her on match-ups.

Come junior high, she made varsity.
Her father objected:
"Ain't putting money on a uniform
for a girl. Besides, your mother
needs help in the kitchen
after school." The brothers
talked him down, ponied up
the uniform fee
out of their hay baling cash.
The coach talked to the old man:
"She's got some skills.
I'll see to it she don't get hurt."
Then he worked her out.
"Man-to-man, like it says.
Their job is to shake you;
yours is to stick.
On your toes. Anticipate.
Get where they're going
before they do."
By the end of the season
he started her on point.
She was a starter
in her sophomore year.
Her dad even came
to some of the games: second half,
after milking was done.

By her junior year they vote her captain.
The brothers switch over
to wrestling, so she works out now
with that other girl player,

skinny forward from town.
All the time, shooting free throws,
drilling lay-ups, spot-up jumpers,
and blocks. The forward, a senior,
starts driving out before the season even starts.
Every weekend, ball and sneakers,
pounding the boards,
quick turns and fakes,
stutter steps, crossovers,
they drill till they drop, sweaty,
muscles limp, tingling,
straw dust clinging
to hot skin and hair.

Until that one Sunday
when the old man,
checking calves down below,
hears the hard play, the grunts
the groans and the laughter.
He climbs up the ladder.
She figures he's come to watch
the contest, the brisk play.
What he sees is dust, sweat,
and contact. Like a horse,
he smells threat in some corner
of his heart. "That's enough.
You tell that coach you're done.
We need help around here.
And you." He turns to the tall forward,
"You stay away from my girl."

Coming Out to Mom

A few years after my divorce,
Mom rides Amtrak in a wide arc
around the American West,
stopping at each station
where her kids live.
His stop: Portland, Oregon.

Even then she may have known
that cancer burned through her kidneys,
her legacy from long marriage
to my father who smoked
till the very end, or would have,
if the nurses had given him
that one more cigarette he begged for
in the nursing home,
oxygen tank there beside his bed.
He died before
the divorce was final.

Two years later, while setting her life
to rights, seeing all the kids but one,
she visits my ex. At some point,
perhaps as the second wife
stepped into the kitchen,
arms laden with dinner plates,
Mom turns to him and asks,
"What went wrong between you two?"
"She's a lesbian," he says, all innocence
and a big wide grin.
 "But, I thought you knew."

MORGAN GRAYCE WILLOW

The Front

I

We turn from one county road
onto another.
After we crest the rise
we see it, the wall
of deep charcoal,
a sharp demarcation,
as if an animated curve leapt
off the weatherman's map
onto the world before us.
It's headed our way.
Pieces of its frayed selvage swirl
along the creek bottom,
forcing willows, maples,
and the one black walnut beside the barn
to writhe, their limbs twisting upon themselves
as if seeking safety beneath their own
lower branches. Whiter sprigs of cloud
shapeshift against the whirling backdrop,
coiling, uncoiling.

We turn back.

By the time we get to the highway,
the torrent is on us.
You drive as one raised among these fields,
steering between lightning flashes
by instinct. I watch the right edge
where the roadway meets the ditch
just as I had from the back seat
when Dad drove through sleet,
Mom beside him, her jaw set tight.

WHEN WE BECOME WEAVERS

II

All afternoon, we have wandered
the paths of our people. In towns
along the Minnesota-Iowa border,
where the largest populations
are in cemeteries, we've found
some of my German folks.
Some of yours, Dutch and Danes,
had been told to follow the Cedar
upriver to Austin, then head west
toward the stand of timber,
the place that would become Albert Lea.

Between ourselves and this lightning,
metal; beneath us, rubber on asphalt.
They had only canvas overhead,
wooden-spoked wheels held
by a thin rim of iron,
and a team of strong oxen,
more afraid of fire
than of rain.

III

The seam at the edge of prairie and sky
lives deep in our cells.
To see that line on a day like today,
undulating, its greens ranging from sharp,
mixed with yellow, to dull and silver-backed,
to see it tossed against that blue
by which all other blues are defined,
to see this interrupted by cumulus, white and occasional,
building and degrading to heather-gray,
then to gunmetal, now to near-perfect black,

MORGAN GRAYCE WILLOW

to see it between light too shocking
for sight, to peer through this shield of rain,
this is to be backed into the elements
of our people's stories.

We go for high ground,
through water coming both down and up,
swirling around tires in this place
that remembers itself as marshland
and longs to return.

Iowa

Many will have you believe
this flatland has nothing to hide.
Her curves are one of many
elements she conceals.

Geodes, the state rock, require damage
to reveal their glisten.

My name rings long across the loess hills,
but no one knows how to call it.

My insteps are the bend of the rivers,
the natural borders between this beautiful
land and the next.
Blooming prairie grass is the hair
falling over my temples.

Lay your cheek against the earth.
Let your hip bones press into the dirt.
Feel the hillock, its slight rise
as if moving to meet you.
Stay in the tall grass until the moon reappears.
Remember this soil carved so long ago
by glaciers. Where I was born,
in the driftless zone of steep
hills and valleys, you'd almost think
you were among mountains.

No one who sees me now knows
the land where my heart was born.

VALERIE WETLAUFER

Pastoral

Desperate men do not make patient women.

This town, these years, always living on the edge of something.

Disease, drought, revival, recession.

The woods are musky, but give way to water.

Fish and stags float when shot dead.

One year there was no rain; the next, rivers overflowed.

Not a hell mouth or hydrophobic, but even the air here is tainted.

The ice never quite crusts over, babies are left untended, crops go missing.

My wife won't quit visiting whores.

Recall the rhyme we sang in school:

For every evil under the sun,
There is a remedy, or there is none.
If there be one, try and find it;
If there be none, never mind it.

Our hands in a circle clapped for every word; we thought we'd smash sin
like a bug.

It hid inside us, coiled, knowing someday we'd stray.

But who's to say which sin is ours? Each time I read your letters, I see
things differently.

Why shouldn't scripture be the same?

Grass caught in our teeth as we laughed, rolling down hills like barrels,
the curves of each
          mound forgiving but spoken for.

There is no remedy for us.

VALERIE WETLAUFER

Call & Response

The Townsfolk

> In case of emergency, we build our fences high,
> our barns sturdy, our women of iron. Our boys
> swim naked in the crick, and train tracks skirt
> our town, carrying trouble away. Dissent,
> liquor, and impurity must be chased down. Worry
> settles like dust in the lines of grandmothers'
> faces. These are troubled times, the ice house
> knowing naught of ice.

Gertrude

> I tried to leave a dozen times,
> but smoke fills the stove.

The Poet

> Two birds sit on a line.
> I watch through my window;
> flapping wings, cawing.
> Sometimes, in profile, they look
> like one large bird. Sometimes
> they are different species altogether.
> Women are like this, when we live
> side by side, years stretched between
> us like laundry. Top and bottom,
> butch and femme, lover and beloved.
> Nothing is static. Everything shared.

> Each contains both birds.

> All things are feral.
> Tame: a myth. Still, our wives want us
> on a leash and leathered.

The Telegrapher

Eighty-eight is code for love and kisses.

Ladies send notes for gingham, plaid, flannel.
Husbands out West wire for cash, and gals
sell their hair and jewels. A visiting opera
singer receives notices from New York City;
urgent obituaries funnel through my fingers.
Dots and dashes intertwine on paper for lovers
far away. A slim-faced tomboy in church dress
weeps on the bench outside. She pays me
with a chicken. Her husband is in jail, and no
lawyer will arrive. Dismay hollows her eyes.

Anna

There are years when nothing happens.

We go on collecting hat pins, dusting stairs.

I've started to wear my ma's clothes.

Mine have all been burned.

I do not usually look so like a girl.

Dogs chew at the hem of such skirts, prairie colored and thick.

So much of my skin is shielded, but it is no remedy.

I cannot put myself right concerning this impulse for you.

At church they tell me Nature is all God's power.

I just go for the hymns.

VALERIE WETLAUFER

The Newspaperman

After the sentence was passed, the smaller woman,
much bereaved, clung to the larger woman's suspenders.
I thought of my own wife, May, how she repeats this action
each morning, stuffing my pencil and paper scraps into my pocket,
guessing the time I'll be home for dinner by the weather
and gossip in the air.

Theft alone isn't news. There is always a story beneath the story.

The Poet

My fiancée and I met with a minister,
who asked what we would do about
money and sex. Fighting about both
was in our future, but then,
solace reigned. We clutched hands,
cut eyes, and our smiles were fluorescent.

Some days I want to roam. I imagine
the peaceful solitude of wind across
a prairie. But left behind, imagining
her voice saying someone else's name,
I know that anger comes first, then lack.

Some mistakes are consciously made.
Others are inevitable; inchoate unions
built on absence and fear.

The Harlot

Frank never stays long,
and never sits
on the bed.
I bend over my dressing table
and watch his eyes
in the mirror. China hands
hug my hips. Teeth

leave their imprint
on my shoulder. Sweat leaks
through my slip, bunched up
at the waist. Even when unruly,
my breasts are hushed doves
beneath his fingers. Rude gent.
In his eyes, the pain of misplacement.

The Cellmate

In life outdoors, I tended roses.
It was my duty to outshine
the cleverness of rabbits
bent on destruction. Inside,
we are the ones subject to treatments.
Our thorns trimmed, vices
corralled. My husband loved
two things: whiskey and
uprooting roses. I am vigilant
when it comes to weeds.
When I used the sheep shears
to trim back thistles, I was
inventive. When I used them
to split open my husband's throat:
a mortal sin. This new cellmate
is a thief. They say she's someone's
husband. I mistrust her glances.
I know what a husband can steal.

The Preacher

The Lord God in his goodness
created us male and female,
and by the sacrament of marriage
founded human community in a joy
that begins now and is brought
to perfection in the life to come.

Brides pledge their troth,
and husbands bid cherish.
I bless their communion, hear
their vows and wish them peace.
In some cases, I shake my head
at the suffering that will surely
follow. Too young, too poor,
too far along already. Nothing
in excess, or you've opened
the door for strife.

Apostle Paul said it is better
to marry than to be aflame.
He saw the difference
between such states.

The Townsfolk

Her hair is a tattered thundercloud
where once her lambskin brow
launched men from trains.

They still tell stories of the widow,
always looking the other way,
watching for that telltale dust
coming up off the road, the signal
that her husband's riding home.

Looking from the front porch
of her homestead far from town
was one thing—the doctor
told the men in the saloon
of her far-off eyes—

but now that Mrs. Blunt lives in town,
she should know she's alone;
that her husband ain't never coming home.

Still she waits for a soft-featured man to return,

dressed in black cheviot suits,
kangaroo calf shoes, her gaze recalling
how his fingertips kissed hers.

The Poet

Women are words to me now.
I dress them like paper dolls,
press their thin faces together
in a kiss. My own divorce is
fresh-faced as Anna out
riding her mare in the snow.

Marriage confounds me.
I am trying to erect a shelter
in which to cache my nerves.
I am trying to tell you a story
of my life: you split the apple
with a knife, held one half up
to my lips. The spilled juice
stained our bed. Whose hand?
Whose lips? Whose dress?

VALERIE WETLAUFER

Heartland

I used to eat dirt, handfuls of fertile black
shoveled into my gaping child's mouth.
At bathtime my mother chided—
she spotted corn growing in my ears—
so soiled they were—and she scrubbed
until the fields were thoroughly plowed.

Stones were the next step, smooth
pebbles I sucked on and swallowed
accidentally, weighing me down,
conspiring with gravity to keep me rooted
in Iowa until I learned that with enough
windspeed and vigorous pumping,

my apterous arms would carry me.

Jack

closes the door turns up the heater we have to idle for four minutes even
though I'm the only one getting on at this stop Patty hasn't been around
for four days mad dad's been gone for two ever since he threw the table
on mom the other kids scream and yell I stare out the window at nothing
the day is a gray blur cold and rainy Katie sits in the seat in front of me
she is in second grade she lives behind me next to the vacant lot she
breathes on the glass fogs it up draws hearts with her fingertip Jack revs
the bus no Patty it's a gray nothing outside I stare the bus jumps forward
then kids yell *Hey! Hey! Bus driver wait!* Jack looks in his long side mirror
the bus sighs then stops some kids are pointing yelling I kneel on my seat
see Patty run down Rose Avenue and then up the bus steps her cheeks
are red her hair is wet stuck back in a pony tail a boy yells *Hey it's P girl*
then the other kids laugh talk they're not interested in Patty the girl who
used to pee in her seat wear stinky clothes Jack nods shuts the door I
stare at her long saggy jeans dark blue zipper sweatshirt white bumper
broken in Reebok tennis shoes

Hey she says slides into my seat *what's happening* her face is red and white
and wet everyone is talking no one is paying attention to her any more
she punches my shoulder it doesn't hurt Patty is back! she puts her hands
into her sweatshirt pockets *Hey* she says again balls her hands up under
her sweatshirt she's nervous stares at the top of the seat in front of us
green padded vinyl in case our heads hit it during an accident I lean on
it the hard padding feels good on my forehead Patty's back! Jack takes a
corner sharp slides Patty into me smashes me against the window Katie's
heart slips makes a jagged line like a V the boys yell *Ewww get off me*

CHRISTINE STARK

Sorry kids Jack waves his hand in the rear view mirror straightens the bus *Shat up* a boy yells from the back Patty's still on top of me past the blonde brick apartment buildings square and flat past the baseball fields past the woods past the pond past the park wet swing sets monkey bars chain link fence gas station insurance company building's sign says *St. Paul Insurance have five minutes stop in we'll drop your price by 25% guaranteed see us for all your needs* Patty's still on top of me I think this must mean she likes me doesn't hate me her hands balled in her sweatshirt pockets

Puddles

in the school parking lot a line of dark orange busses wet creepy crawling kids like swarming bees Patty's squishing me *Stay in your seats until we reach the front* Jack holds his hand up brakes idles everyone sits on the edges of the seats Patty doesn't move I don't move the bus lurches idles lurches idles Patty takes her left hand out keeps it in a ball puts it on her leg *Stupid idiot* someone yells Patty unfolds her fingers puts her hand on my leg *Dink* someone shouts *Hey* Jack yells lifts his hand Patty grabs my hand holds it tight *All right everyone off* Jack opens the door it cuts in half slides apart before I know what I'm doing I grab Patty kiss her on the cheek her hand pokes me in the stomach all the other kids are in the aisle pushing to get out the cold air rushes in *Lezzies dykes look at that gays freaks fags look at that a girl kissed another girl!*

OHHHHHHH!!!! all the girls yell they don't touch our seat when they walk by they lean away from us my hands drop down I stare at the seat think oh no Patty looks out the window it's raining in straight lines the other kids are yelling laughing grossing out they run onto the playground *P girl and the fifth grade girl kissed they're lezzies dykes fags freaks!*

I put my forehead on the seat oh no I don't know what I just did Patty doesn't say anything did I do something bad does she think so *C'mon girls* Jack says looking at us in the rear view mirror *I don't know what just happened but you need to get off the bus*

CHRISTINE STARK

Jump

in a puddle Patty says and stomps with two feet flat footed sprays mud
water all over the slide all the other kids are inside *Let's go!* and so we do
we run Rocky style our fists in the air *Yo Adrian!* around the outside of
the school we spy around the corners our bodies pushed up against the
brick we spy looking for teachers and janitors and hall monitors we move
slow we are sneaky then fast Patty makes a pose Bruce Jenner I laugh
like it's California sun on my face like I know nothing else but happiness
like Payne Avenue is not one block away like mad dad is dead mom and
me live in an apartment somewhere like me and Patty will be together
best friends forever and ever I love her long saggy jeans Bruce Jenner
muscles I laugh like mad dad won't smash the night time whip me hit me
break me I laugh and laugh and laugh Patty's cheeks dark wet sweatshirt
ducking running spying I laugh like there is nothing else in all the world
nothing else in all the world! but me and Patty and the puddles wet mud
on the cuffs of our jeans we're late for school and we laugh like there is
nothing else in all the world but us

CHRISTINE STARK

Yo Adrian!

my fists in the air rain hits our faces gray day cold day we're late for
school day Patty's shoes are muddy n wet her cheeks are rose red her
breath comes out of her mouth like lace she grabs me pushes me against
the school bricks bite into my head but I don't care she holds me rain in
lines from the sky Patty holds me she kisses me her breath on my lips

Let's go she whispers *Okay* I say her lips and cheeks rose red we are
Bruce Jenner! we are Martina Navratilova! we are Ahmad Rashad Fran
Tarkington Muhammad Ali float like a butterfly sting like a bee fists
above our heads Rocky Balboa style I am Rocky! *Yo Adrian I love you!*
we run across the playground around the slide through the swings push
them high in the air the other kids are in school we run the cuffs on our
jeans are wet they hit our ankles we don't care! we run faster than anyone
has ever run before *Yo Adrian! I love you!* faster than anyone has ever run
before over the sidewalk across the baseball field red thick sand on our
shoes we run over left field into the trees black trees dark trees wet trees
trees with wet black skin they stand over us with curled branches we run
our feet move our muscles are strong laughing where are we going I don't
know I don't care we run we breathe listen to our breath listen to our
breath listen to our breath

we run under the trees to the other side me and Patty away from school
the laughing kids *dykes fags freaks* we bend over our breath knitting
together I can do anything the strongest person in all the world when
I'm with Patty my best friend forever and ever we laugh high five like
she scored a goal I made a save nothing can break us apart me and Patty
stand then we run laugh breathe like there is nothing in all the world but
us

CHING-IN CHEN

Blueprint

                                              The day
                                    you cross the line,

                              somebody else's ideas. I give

              us to hold ourselves –
        two stories, red-faced

                    Navigation, meridians.   Measurements:
                    width of foot, length of body I left in
                    rooms. Between mine and hers. High-
                    est point of prosperity. Under sand, un-
                    der subway, which tunnels leading to doors
                    opening.

                                        taking to bed before dusk

                                              my government
                                        name, form a path

        self-preservation.

                                              with my mouth
                                    makes an alternative vein.

        You begin saying
        sorry all the way.

                    I do not want   *Some sugar to*
        follow.

Heritage

When   *"To say"* a woman

become monument *"in front of all these people"*
                                never sang

                        porridge songs
or pulled   by my hair
into line
                        she placed me row by row   *"men and boys"*
black heads *"surging"*   uncovered production
            "in knots of half a dozen or more"

I became not her stone
"who have paid money for their wives"

she *"reckless"*   stood tremble   in the fire
                                                        "get a rope"

the crowdface   *"regular traffic"*
"black with people"   stared her down
"the little mite"   corridor   *"a good many times"*
                                        "the unprintable"

"sneak[ing]"
                                        "advance a foot"

                        *"string

        them up
to a lamp

post"*

CHING-IN CHEN

Four hours before departure.

I enlist the mother in the expedition. She brings tongue cakes from across the Pacific. While she photographs the Marriott complex, I break the plastic open. Three addresses now swallowed up by three crunches, three corporations. Next, the Google map says, soap factory, Amtrak station, post office. They're in fact shaped like tongues, are not sweet, not made out of any tongue. The smoking corner man, says WE Energies when I ask him to identify our location. I'm disappointed in the taste. His shirt says, Harley Davidson. The other corner man owns a violet-hatted dog. No lefts here— one way forward against the traffic, against history.

1884-1913.

Dear unknown foot setter. Dear lonely rat eater. Dear cook visiting as a Wisconsin State Fair stove company product demonstrator. Dear lonely 16 hours and six days. Dear lonely deed of a heathen. Dear does not believe in advertising. Dear lonely rat eater. Dear good people are you aware. Dear lonely opium addict. Dear 3,000 men in 12 hours. Dear damage. Dear municipal court. Dear joss house display. Dear Immanuel Presbyterian church missionaries. Dear colored shirts. Dear night shirts. Dear feast of apple pie with roast chicken, beef and pork. Dear hired carriages, dear chosen picnic ground—Union Cemetery. Dear rare day of leisure. Dear fancy goods and teas. Dear "enticing," dear "immoral purposes," dear public anger. Dear March 11, 1889.

CHING-IN CHEN

War

Sister in-between, danger [orange]. Hips sway, feet stomp [gold rush]. I listen

remember that sound. lightning. I practiced

hissing, we form

boat in night, we become

cutting myself

jaguar. What kind of correction mob [which direction] forms vigilante.

Strung wire *in half.* [watching eyes].

> **Somebody else's ideas.** Before me, a body rang with a curling voice, island milk, oil splatter. Were you easy and burnt, were you one and two, light on the feet, never settled in a basket, your mother a breath that was taken by sea, by land, by freight.

[is it safe?] if we quiet, [another envious morning after]

what does the heart sit high
amongst lights watch other
bodies pass but the end path
a lonely and who
wants rise
bear her own
weight under the rain

The unit must survive. Drawing in sunrise, call to obey, who is wild. *I say,*
all paths begin here in water.

I say, this is what I learned—

Girl on synthetic girl, push me down to dirt. Mating ritual [braid,
stomach, hair follicle,

to grow silence

metal, something to last
sliding hands] begin.

CRYSTAL BOSON

truck month

in the month of march we give thanks
to our good Ford F-350
who much like that fella Jesus
is so fuckin tired of our shit
but still kinda loves us and works
despite our good intentions cause
its his fuckin job

the metaphysics of nigger hating

back then we knew us better
they learned to fear
all in their neckbones
less they congregate in trees
they knew they all had one name
to darken up our door
but we've seen a change of days
now they wet up all our daughters
now they eye up all our sons
now they roll our name all comfort
round their unfamiliar tongues
so let us do the work of the day

CRYSTAL BOSON

seriously, pray for rain

now we can't remember rain
the baked mud of lips knows
all eighty-eight ways
to hex a back flaying sun
God, i don't remember rain
i do not have the skill
to conjure up tears with
the day's thumbs all in my eyes
my tongue has grown dry
and too useless for prayer
my palms have turned fallow
and push off from the plow
my legs have quick withered
and fold down like the grass

God responds to rick perry and his national day of prayer in a language he can understand

boy, ya'll were gonna get rain
but you done flapped your gums
now grass gotta die hot
tongues'll flounder all about mouths
I had scheduled up rain
now I'm spending my day
scrubbin' your voice from my ear
and clenchin up the assholes of clouds

JES BRAUN

Family Tree

Pop-pop

Drank a lot. Only missed two days of work in his 40 years on the job.
Never missed a day of drinking. He was a blur at the bottom of the
staircase as a child. The split level house was split. He had the basement. I
was scared of his bathroom.

Na-Na

Sometimes, I catch people wearing her perfume and I simultaneously get
happy and upset that someone would steal her smell like that. She was
good to me. I was afraid to sleep alone in her house with her because I
was scared of what was in her closets at night. Nothing. Nothing was in
her closets except closety things. But at night at her house I just stared at
the doors with my eyes glued open.

Grandpa

He is a hospital bed. I didn't know him. People say that I am like him.
My wit, my love of numbers. He is a body in a bed. Time spent in an
old nursing home. I would play outside, or sit in the lobby and stare
at a copper tree filled with names. They unplugged him after double
pneumonia.

Grandma

She cut the crusts of my sandwiches to feed the birds. She knit sweaters
for babies. Did page after page of crossword puzzles. She sat alone in a
house. She planted trees for every grandchild. She visited grandpa daily.
Later she would stop feeding herself and soon I was visiting her and the
copper tree and then there were no more visits.

Nick (1/2 brother)

He was half of me. 4 years older and father-less. He was always getting hurt. He was brilliant. He had a baby girl too early. Drugs too early. Jail too early. Another baby girl. He's working it out.

Nick's Dad

He was a fling for my mom. She was newly 18. Nick the fetus, the zygote, dropped in on them and when my mom told him, he asked her to marry him. She laughed at him. He split town the next day. She never saw or heard from him again.

Caleb (Dad's girlfriend's son)

My dad wasn't easy on him. He had trouble taking pills. His mom used to mash up his A.D.D. medication in a cup to give to him. He was handsome. He had anger problems. He has a baby boy now. His girlfriend was a meth baby. She takes pills. Anything she can find. Their baby is on feeding tubes. He will never walk. He has Caleb's face.

Cady (Dad's girlfriend's daughter)

I chased her down once. I was angry at her. Chased her down the length of the trailer, into her room, jumped on top of her in our bunk beds. She was shaking, frozen, terrified. I held my hand above her midsmack and then looked at her and crumbled. I've never raised my hand again.

Cady was a beautiful baby, then a gorgeous child. By nine, our phone never stopped ringing for her. By eleven, she lost her virginity behind our trailer. By sixteen, she was pregnant. That baby was taken away from her. She beat her boyfriend. She has three babies now. Twins too. Her new boyfriend hits her.

JES BRAUN

Ellen (Dad's girlfriend)

She has amazing eyes. Like the earth. And freckles. Her first husband, Caleb and Cady's Dad, beat her mercilessly. There was a miscarriage, somewhere. She once tackled her mother's boyfriend. He had a knife to her mother. Had her mom pinned to the bed. She never tackled my father. He would smack her around the basement, when they had a basement. And then around the trailer. Punch her back, sit on her. Now, she works a minimum wage job and laughs a lot. Comes home and sleeps a lot. They love each other. I see it.

Dad

He struggles. He drinks a lot. He's bad with money. Pop-pop hit him. He hit others. He hates it. He hits us and then comes back and cries. And wants to hold us. He is two people. He is four people. He's my dad. He would lecture for hours. You never knew when he would switch back to being angry. When he would cry. When he would lash out. When he would hold us. I love him so much my heart hurts.

Mom

She was wild. She was fun. She was young. We moved every couple months. I went to so many different elementary schools. She left when I was eight, to go on the road with her new rocker husband. He was a ginger. They broke up 10 years later. She lost her spark. Lost her teeth. Got lost in meth. Ditto the love and hurt heart thing.

Girls, Girls, Girls.

June. Kate was June. Kate was my first major girl relationship. When we kissed the first time, there was a pulse behind my eyes and blinding flashes and I thought *Oh Jesus Christ, I am seeing fireworks.* Kate. Kate was bad news, but Kate. Thank you Kate, you opened the flood gates.

Riley. Riley was **July.** Riley had glasses, sinewy limbs and bow lips that made me bite my own to prevent myself from biting hers. The first time Riley and I kissed, we had climbed up the underside of the Lake Street bridge that yawns over the Mississippi River. A raucous thunder storm descended upon us and the river quaked from the pelting rain. I tackled Riley underneath that bridge, kissing her as a beer rolled over the edge and turned end over end, smashing into the river.

With **August** came Baby Dyke. I was at the neighbor's playing gay spin-the-bottle when the girl sitting next to me ran her hand up my back, and then down my arm, my stomach, my thigh. I looked at her, slightly cross-eyed and we grabbed each other's hand and ran away from the game, up the sixty-seven steps to my apartment. Slugging whiskey, we tore at each other's clothes, cracking my eye glasses into pieces when we rolled over them. Later, when we bumped into my roommate in the hallway, I found out that this girl, this hot, now blurry, girl, was a senior in high school.

September and **October** brought the rockabilly co-op girl. We would stay up late, drinking Black Label and fighting her cat for bed space. Unfortunately, the co-op girl fell in love with her co-op co-worker in a terrible co-op way. Rainbow Foods sales of organic bananas soared for a month following my co-op breakup.

Co-op girl was out, but she left in her wake a flannel of new lesbian friends.

JES BRAUN

Bennie. Bennie was the first of the flannel. We met again at a gay girl dance night in **November**. She was tiny, wirey, had buzzed hair and wore little boys' Star Wars t-shirts. I found myself at four in the morning naked on a stranger's couch, Bennie between my legs. She wooed me with surprise and disgust that co-op girl would give me up.

December came in and Bennie ran back to her ex-girlfriend. For the rest of December, I dated whiskey.

January came. Bennie and her ex became exes again. One oppressive winter night, whiskey intimately introduced me to Bennie's ex. Four hours later, ex, I, and one other were pushing each other's thighs apart. What a tiny dyke world.

February and **March**, I dated my school books. I spooned them, cried on them, hugged them close to my chest.

April brought Baby Dyke 2: Revenge of Tiny Hormones. The second Baby Dyke was slightly out of the high school age range. She whisked in fervidly and out the same way. She opened the door for May.

Drunken decisions and envious pool playing abilities had me waking up next to Miss **May**. The sex was amazing, went on for days. I was falling for her until Miss May's secret ingredient turned out to be methamphetamine.

But **June**, oh June, back around again. June brought motorcycle girl. Motorcycle girl hooked me with her sanity, her motorcycle, swishy hair, her bow lips. I am a sucker for bow lips. Motorcycle girl is now my motorcycle girlfriend and closes the calendar on my dating year.

This is an open letter to you:

Fuck you.
Fuck you and your nicotine stained fingers.
I used to worry. Sometimes. I used to worry about my shape. My legs.
Are they too muscular? Is my belly too round?
I wasn't worried about being too big when you came up behind me.
I didn't even know you were there. THAT IS THE WORST PART …
ididn'tevenknowyouwerethere
The hallway at work was dark. It was always dark. I could see the kitchen
of the bar at the end. Glowing. I was mid-step. I was lost in thoughts.
And then you.
I felt you grab me from behind. Pull me backwards.
And your hands.
Your hands spanned the width of me. Your fingertips dug into me. I felt
your frame wrap around me. Engulf me from behind.
I didn't worry about being too muscular then… Too round…
I was too small…
I felt your body curl into me. Your acrid breath in my hair, my ear.
And then your hands. Your dirty fucking hands. You scooped them up
under my skirt.
And then your fingers. Your fingers were there. In me. Inside of me.
And I screamed.
I screamed and pushed against you. Screaming NO! NO!
Tripping.
Falling towards the gaping kitchen door.
And then you laughed.
And turned away.
10 seconds you had your fingers on my body. In my body.
10 seconds.
Fuck you.

Mother.

Long limbed, swayed back. Mother. Arms reaching, arms pulling.
Mother. Cigarette smashed between her lips, baby on the hip, Mother.
Mother laughing, baby in the crib, baby on the step. Mother. Mother
bounding down the steps. Mother late for work. Mother. Baby
straightening out. Baby reaching out, for Mother. Mother working
late. Baby at the gate. Up so very late, Mother. Mother on the couch,
bouncing baby about. Mother. Mother combing baby's hair, crying on the
chair, Mother.

Poor White Girls

Trapped her in a shed
with a black snake,
she said,
for what seemed like
hours, letting the black
penetrate her memory
and down in between
her special place that
wasn't so special anymore.

"I dunno what was
worse," she said. "That—
or everyone letting it
happen."

"Mmm-hmm," the other
said. And we all nodded
a knowing head.

We pass joints and
stories and
glances.

The other took her teeth
out to eat, wrapped them
gently in a napkin,
covered her mouth with
her hand between each
bite. She left the front
ones in a room, in a
little house, where she
was locked, tortured, her
life's life beside her and
another inside.
The man passed out
long enough

for each to
escape through the window-
          dropping two stories.
Dropping and losing the
son inside.

I try not to stare
at the blank space she covers.

Instead, I focus on the
smoke in my lungs. Holding
it there, letting
it grasp all the sadness
and exhale into the
collective cloud above our
heads.

"I hate love songs," I
tell them. "I hate
hearing them and thinking
of him." I don't say
it, but they know I
mean my father.

          "That must have really
          given you a skewed
          view about love." My
          therapist told me.

No shit—

I thought, but said nothing.

"That's why I only date
women," they say
and laugh at the
simultaneous remark.
          As if a woman couldn't
          break my heart;

as if she, the first one,
had not. And for
a man, a man who
ate her up, swallowed whole,
and shat her out without
a bit of remorse.

"I'm gonna roll another
one," I say and they nod.
"Sick of these flashbacks,"
I say and they nod.

I roll it, I light it, I tell
them the latest memory.

I tell them that I was
in a cage and I see
his snake skin boots: tan,
glistening in the moon
light and I hear
children crying and I
smell fear. I see
his boots and I screech
like a cat, like an
owl, claws out, ready
to attack.

"And that's it." I say.

They nod and
pass joints and
knowing glances.

NATALIE J. BYERS

Rumors

We go for her birthday, the six of us,
to the gay bar on the corner.

She says she wants to dance and
stare at the drag queens and "Aren't
the queens so hot? It's like the
best of both worlds."

Settled with our drinks: screwdrivers,
we pass small talk, share pictures
of our kids, complain about how
fat we've gotten.

The Host Queen hollers:
        "Where are all my gay people at?"
And half the room whoos.
        "Where are all my straight people?"
And the other half whoos.
        "What about my bis? Where are you?"

"Whoohoo!" I scream and realize that
I am the only one who made a sound. I hear
whispers, "She must be confused."
I feel the eyes staring, mouths giggling.

I look at my five companions and they are
staring, too. I ask if I have embarrassed them and
I am pissed that I have to ask.

But my head tells me to screw these
assholes and dance. So I do, but no one wants to
dance with the confused bi-girl. I dance

with the speaker, let the bass vibrate
through my hands and down into, down into,
down into my body.

Lesbian Thoughts

She binds her chest
But still has breasts underneath
The neighborhood kids call her a pussy
I guess you are what you eat
And as her conscience
I encourage her to speak
She ain't a winner in the streets
So in her mind she'll be boxing me
Self expression ain't for you honey
Hold your words and grit your teeth
And your reflection don't take vacations
Because hate doesn't sleep
Tomboys stay buried under baggy clothes
So in the closet is where you'll find me
So with this piece hi to the new you
And the old: **Rest In Peace**

To live & die in L.A.
Some followers are mindless
So repeat everything I say
Lesbianism offends masculinity
So some cultures reinstate corrective rapes
Feminists have theories so continue to ride the waves
Kicked out at seventeen
So your home is where your head lays
Yell revolution and
Ninjas get ghost like finger-waves
Self-identity is priceless
And real poetry doesn't pay
If vagina monologues are *better than chocolate*
Then all real poets are prophets
Straight women play for both teams
So male producers continue to make profit

JESSICA VERSE GABRIELLE

And as Amy's "Tears Dry on Their Own"
She stands drenched in a puddle
I'm tryna paint a picture
Don't take this as being subtle
Hate crimes trespass
So victims find trouble
It's just V, Nikki, & Baldwin standing in a huddle
You see I drink Molotov cocktails out of beer bottles
And continue to search for messages in a bottle
Stone Butch Blues because I bottle my emotions
Knowledge is a death sentence
So I guess I'll die putting it all out in the open

Pride

"I can understand why you want a divorce now
Though I can't let you know it,
Pride won't let me show it
Pretend to be heroic, that's just one to grow with
But deep inside a Ninja ..."
Forget it!
I think I'm in love like Beyonce be with Jigga
Heard the song plenty but I still can't cry you a river
I love her but tears I just can't give her
In the midst of an argument, I lost sight of the mission
Pride is the perpetrator
And my girl is the victim
I have an addiction
Now that you know
Don't ask me why I'm twitching
(shhh it itches)
Caught the ball
But now I'm having a hard time pitching
Listen! Lauryn Hill is truly genuine
She said "Verse don't be a hard rock
When you really are a gem"
Real women have curves
And your pride is paper thin
I can't love her so father I've committed a sin
Pass me a bottle of gin
And let me tell you them
 I just wrote this and I'm having a hard time listening
Dancing around the question like Alv and em
Instead of expressing my problems
Like a mistress I sleep with them
But like Shaq tryna make a free throw
The issue is above the rim

JESSICA VERSE GABRIELLE

A whore and pride is my pimp
The metaphor is ill
But yall I think I'm just sick
I was tryna see love from a certain angle and missed it
I'm addicted to the distance
Respect won't let me call you a bitch
So I'm stuck in the gym trying to reach a level of fitness
Pride seduces me "hit this"
Too much emotion
I won't allow myself to be that open
Some would say I'm just focused
Put me on a cloud of ego and now I'm floating
A tub full of tears and now I'm soaking
Pride but no Prejudice
I know, I know it's thought provoking
Pride is the reason my emotions are claustrophobic
In the closet is where they hide
Pride dehydrates me
That's why I can't cry
To avoid issues it keeps me high
Gives me angel wings so now I can fly
You might see too much if you look into my eyes
My mind was decapitated so you might see flies
Referred to as an Oreo
So you might see white lies
Was caught smuggling tears in on the side
Entered a not guilty plea
I guess I'm in denial
Sadistic so you might find a smile
At the end of the trial
The judge ruled by way of Fergie big girls don't cry
Escort dignity in, love Goodbye

Sai (Say) Intro

I'm so intro like hello
Crazy, copasetic, but mellow
Singing plantation lullabies call it Ndegeocello
LaLaLaLaLaLa Carmelo
I rock to heart beats and an occasional cello
While passing stories and wild grass in meadows
Riot and protest
I like to politically meddle
Arming myself with pencils and metal
Pigs armed occupation ninja what medals?
Unapologetic my discomfort won't allow me to settle
Efforts of peace disguised as a feast Black Kettle
Yeah I'm *Tour de Francing* it with no pedals
Never selling out but I peddle
Using earthly resources
I blow dust and toss pebbles
And my ex never learned to properly let go
It's like trying to convince a honorary white
Who only sees yellow
Or wanting a child but your stomach won't grow
So baby let the tears flow
Because I'm so outro like let's go

Tyra

Alone
Despite the people gathered close
Cold
Despite the warm blood pumping out
Farce
Despite the seriousness of her condition
Dying
Despite the EMTs kneeling by her

She
died from prejudice, not from injuries
She
bled out across the hot, black asphalt
She
heard the laughter and I wonder, did
She
know it was her saving angels laughing?

EMTs
angels brought on swift steel wings
EMTs
trained to act with speed and grace
EMTs
disturbed by what they do not approve
EMTs
bigoted and cruel turn fallen angels

Trans* Love

::feeling dysphoric and unlovable; feeling out of place with gender; feeling alone::

The mirror is an enemy. It reflects lies. I can't look like that; it's not what I see when I close my eyes. I see smooth, clear skin and long, wavy, ginger hair. I see a face unmarred by time and the ravages of testosterone poisoning. I see me and I am beautiful. But the mirror reflects someone else. It shows a middle aged man in a dress with limp, thinning hair. The mirror shows a scarred and weathered face, five o'clock shadow and cheeks sunken from anxiety and radical diets. The mirror, my reflection, is an abusive partner. It shows what I hate and makes me want to self harm.

::picking up the sterilized shard of glass set aside for this::

It is easy to picture the cut, performed with surgical steadiness. First it will just seem to be a line. Slowly, blood will bead on the line as my pulse causes it to seep out the sliced skin. I will watch it. The beading will become a rivulet, the rivulet will run down my arm, the blood will drop in perfectly circular splashes onto the hospital white countertop.

It would be gorgeous.

::dialing your number::

Three, four, five rings. Voicemail.

::wanting to leave a message but not sure what to say::

A tone. A breath. A long pause.

::hanging up::

The phone rings; it's you.

::hesitating::

JENNIFER-RIVER ELLER

Three, four, five. The call goes to voice mail.

Immediately it rings again.

::answering::

It is you. Concern colors your voice. I try to explain how I feel, but the words are jumbled and twisted. They abuse each other, consume rationality and meaning.

::crying::

Your voice is soft, kind. You are on your way.

::sinking to the floor; making my six foot one inch frame small and impenetrable::

You use your key and find me pressed against the counter. You kneel beside me and wrap your arms about me. They are stronger than they were six months ago and the hair is thicker, coarser. You run the back of your hand along my cheek, wiping away tears.

::gazing at you::

Your face is thinner and more angular. Your pores are larger and patches of brown hair are visible on your cheeks and chin. The brown fuzz overwhelms me with a dizzying combination of lust and dysphoria. You smile and my heart melts.

You stand, all awkward charm and help me to my feet. I sway a little from vertigo and you catch me around my waist. With tenderness, being careful not to cut me or yourself, you open my hand and take the glass shard. You set it back in its case and close the lid. You would never throw it out and that is one of the reasons I love you.

You guide me to the bathroom and start the shower, adjusting it to that perfect temperature of steamy, tolerable, scalding. Heat burns the dysphoria off. As the mirror fogs, you unbutton your shirt and drape it across the laundry hamper. You slip out of your shoes and shed your slacks and boxers. You stand before me in nothing but your binder. You give me a moment to take your tan, handsome body in, before slipping my blouse and bra off. They are deposited in the hamper, along with my skirt and the pantyhose I cut the legs off to secure my tuck.

::sighing; helping you remove your binder::

We step into into the shower. It scalds. I take the pain into my heart, storing it away as pleasure to be reflected on and relished. You caress my double A breasts; cupping them in your small but powerful hands. You kiss my nipples.

::sighing; massaging your clit-cock::

You moan, you kiss my neck. You slide your hands down my side and between my legs.

::shivering in anticipation::

You slip two fingers into the soft, pink flesh of my scrotal sack, fingering a make-shift vagina. You gently knead the soft tissue while kissing the spot where I will eventually have cleavage.

::shuddering; weeping; climaxing beneath your loving touch::

I do not grow hard and do not come, I have not done so in several months—this is the only reason I can let you touch me—but I do climax. It is an internal tingling that pulses out from my core, enveloping my whole being. It is blinding in its intensity and I crumple into your waiting arms.

We hold each other as the searing water cascades over us, burning away everything we are not.

C. BETH LOOFE

aiming at the earth

in 1967 the cow and the moon signed a treaty
never to fire rockets upon the earth.
the dish laughed, with justice and joy,
as the fork and the spoon taught blacks and whites
how to embrace their love with marriage.
and they put you into a padded cell in omaha, nebraska
because a rich man's daughter wanted you to kiss her.
this was grim.
this was no fairy tale.
california was dachau for the queer,
but it didn't just happen there.
cutting skin, brains, cutting souls.
calling it science.
better to maim him.
better to make her peas and carrots.
better to kill us dead than to let us be.
sweet faced fresh,
at home that's all you were,
caught unwillingly in dresses you didn't want to wear,
hair plaited in tresses you didn't want to share with the outside world.
outside in.
just trying to be what you'd always been.
so many people afraid of the young man you were meant to be.
sincere, good—no threat, no travesty.
but they took you from your family.
stuck you in a 6x6 concrete psych ward cell 12 blocks off dodge street,
telling you night after night,
"it's all right, baby, you don't *need to be a man*,
you just *need* a man."
daylight didn't bring better.
rotten breath wrapping hell threats of horror to your mother.
you had never done the things they accused you of.
never thought the thoughts they framed you with.
that rich man's daughter lied.
and it was unjust, and you tried to tell them,

C. BETH LOOFE

but no one listens to a poor girl
who looks like a poor boy
who has nothing.
stripped of your rights, your dignity, your clothing,
left only with your tears.
finally,
you cried.
cried at the pictures.
when the group therapy ended.
when the films were over.
when the doctors left your room.
screamed when the shocks left your skin.
they 'offered' you medications.
operations to fix you.
you were not broken.
not broken.
tears trickling down young boyish cheeks,
shaking shoulders thin not weak.
and they honestly would not break you.
not honestly.
then, transgender was transitional.
if you were, you better not be.
they'd just as soon kill you as let you exist.
it was dangerous to resist.
a death sentence to resist must longer.
so when that kind hearted nurse pulled you into a whispering shadowed
hallway
and whispered a way out,
dishonest but neat?
you didn't ask her to repeat it.
44 years later, choking back broken glass cut throat regret,
holding back indignation too proud to scream its way back in,
you piece out a survivor's story to me like a shattered mirror falling up.
the cow and the moon look down from the sky,
and listen.
offer you their treaty and wish you peace.
transgender is not transitional.
in 1967, 12 blocks off dodge street,
you were the young man you were meant to be.

C. BETH LOOFE

i want your children

have you heard?
it's gotten around, though it's taken a while,
i'm a dangerous pedophile!
i eat small, no wait...
large...
no wait...
all children for breakfast lunch and dinner.
for i am a homosexual!
that special kind of sinner,
not safe around the kinder.
injecting fear around them...
my devouring leers around them...
hoping to recruit, destroy, use ploys to get them.
whether eight or eighteen, there is no stopping what
i wont do to defile corrupt or seduce them into my malicious,
chosen lifestyle.
that's what those nebraska republicans say
and i pray, it's true...
i do want your children.
i want them...
...to be honorable.
like that one lanky teenage kid last summer,
who called this asian boy a chink?
i stopped my walk, crossed the street and politely made him
think about what he was saying.
in ear shot of his friends.
oh, it's true what they say.
i was a big scary lesbian that day
who wants your children...
...to be safe.
like the 9 year old who fell off his bike a few yards into the trail.
no one seemed to hear his wailing,
or want to get involved enough
in a possible lawsuit to soothe him,
to wipe the blood off his banged up knees,

put his bike in the trunk,
call his parents and take him home.
it was too much of a risk.
maybe when you've been taking risks just to breathe a breath in an honest
life,
they become easy to inhale.
try it.
but breathing isn't enough. i'm hungry.
i want your babies...
...to be clothed and fed and led in the right direction.
so i will spend my own money to feed your child
because you sold your wic to get your kicks off alcoholic benders,
defend her against midnight invasions from abusive boyfriends
you gave our address to,
three weeks into the weekend babysitting favor
we agreed to.
it's illegal for cohabitating dykes in nebraska to be foster parents,
did you forget that?
i would remind but i am too busy to be interrupted.
i must focus on corrupting the children.
exposing them to bad things, like good character, philosophy and poetry.
teaching them how to read the bible, dr. seuss and silverstein.
empowering them to survive hatred and bigotry.
feeding them sometimes.
breakfast, lunch and dinner.
and if i still sound like a pedophile,
some kind of degenerate sinner,
i've got no more time for you,
trying to change your mind
when i could be helping them grow theirs.
after all, you're right.
i do want your children.

C. BETH LOOFE

what i am

i am a woman.
i am not cute.
i am not a skinny little thing,
sporting hip huggers and tommy girl.
my hair does not flip for the patriarchy.
and it does not curl.
i am not young,
and although i am able to properly consume my opportunities,
the world is not my oyster.
what i am, is a woman, set firmly in the middle of my life.
i am your lover, your sister, a dyke.
i am thick. fat,
i am strong,
and the strength of my thighs will keep you still.
or the strength of my will.
guaranteed.
i am generous.
i am not about greed
fables, stereotypes or labels.
i am an inspiration.
your goal.
i sing to your soul, to your kiss, your bliss…
my touch softens steel.
i am a muse.
let me amuse you.
let me inspire you.
quench your desire.
you game?
play.
play me,
what i am.
a woman.

Down Low Brothers…(night), Part 2

He just left/my night just began
A night/ like many other

Nights/ but this night felt
Different/ yes Ed Gordon is

Serving up a re-hashed AIDS
Show on BET/ it's the day after

World AIDS Day/ but the message/
The message is still relevant/

Black women are contracting
HIV/AIDS at an alarming rate

And still he drives home to her
And he won't tell her that

His car was just parked in my garage/
As he pulls up to the front door

His mind is on me/Flowetry, and it's all right
"i been checking you for a while, your lips, your eyes, your smile"

Words he whispered when we made love/
This man loves music/ music is the gift he gave me

He loves clothes/
Has them tailored by the best in Minneapolis

He subscribes to the Robb Report/ and
His travels take him around the world

ANDREA JENKINS

Paris is in fact where we plan to go
One day/ he will come to terms with the plain truth

That denying his maleness/ created this male mess
And love me in the light.

Working Hands

Daddy was only 15 when he first met 'ol man Rothchilds
his daddy would send him down there with two dollars
and a note to buy a pint of Old Granddad, after awhile
he would borrow some of the jazz recordings that scratched
out of the Motorola hi-fi in the corner near the Bali-Hai
display in the window.
"Ezell, I heard you got that girl upstairs pregnant, you gonna
need a job to take care of that baby" the ol' man said one day;
it was the only square job he ever had. He played his own riff,
not unlike the Jazz idols of his day
Billie, Bird, Miles, Mingus
his eyes in full possession of an all knowingness
that this square job/this square life would never
fit the image he had for himself.

He wandered in and out of this world, poppy induced
dreams, delusions some might say, he played one
syncopated note on top of a blues rhythm
but no one was listening.

I spent the better part of a day staring at the grainy
fading shadows on this early generation Polaroid snapshot of my father
at his first job at Rothchilds' Liquor store, stacking
cases of Pabst Blue Ribbon, Old Milwaukee
and of course the "King of Beers" on black and white
linoleum squares.

To the point that I couldn't
distinguish whether it was his long fingers or mine
clutching the cold steel handle of the wooden freezer
door as if it were the opening to another place, a higher
state of grace, free from contradiction.

ANDREA JENKINS

Mama Calls Me Anna

At the mall I can hear the children
"Daddy, is that a man or a lady?"
My mama just smiles and says her name is Anna

The sagging boys with their jeans hangin'
off their asses shout "fuckin faggots"
and after the bars close they want to lay
and play, I keep my head up though 'cause mama calls me Anna

When pain is the key that unlocks
the door I remind myself that
mama calls me Anna

On birthday wishes
and Christmas greetings—
"To Anna, with love, Mom."

She might not realize that the confidence
she taught me as a little boy helped
me become the woman I am
today.

Neighbor as Self in Mandan, North Dakota

It was all fun and games until their youngest was hit by a truck. We were the lesbian poet moms in the rambling blue farmhouse with the peace sign on one corner; they were the careful Christians in the classic yellow Victorian on the other. There was a mutual keeping of distance, a joint appreciation of the asphalt between us. Their daughter walked over each summer to invite ours to Vacation Bible School, which was thoughtful but annoying, as was the conversion van—get it?—that they parked in our favorite spot. I'm sure they had their issues too, like Lucinda Williams swearing from our windows, the way we'd let the weeds grow with the wildflowers, how our dog approached their dog in a not-so-Christ-like manner. Then their son's skull cracked, and we stopped thinking about parking.

JULIE GARD

On Scarcity

We are short a pair of brown shoes in our house. My partner put them on this morning and I'd already dressed in brown pants, striped socks and a nice green shirt; all I needed were the shoes she was already wearing. I can't believe she took them off. I can't believe I asked her to. It's true they're mine, but I would cut out a kidney for her, even a lung, and so why not give her a shoe? They are perfectly wide and comfortable. She is older, smarter, and doesn't have as many nightmares. We should have better boundaries, at least different-sized feet. We should plan better. She says that it happens on Thursdays. There is something about the end of the week when everything starts running out.

Carnal Struggle, 2006

There's no way to win in bed, in dreams. You
can only lie beside me making love to a U.S.
president who repulses you, while I pluck goose
poop from a nylon car seat. In reality, your
foot is sweet against mine. The dog between
us scratches all night, making wounds where
there were none. This indelible life.

JULIE GARD

Ticks

In the North Woods in June, you learn to write
with ticks crawling up your legs. You go on
with conversation, pick them off in the middle
of sentences, hold them tightly between thumb
and forefinger, up to four at a time. You check
the dog and mistake his vestigial nipple for a
tick. There is one close to his privates and you
pluck it gently, crooning. You've never found one
on you full, only searching, ascending, seeking
the perfect plot of skin. They take so long to
dig in, you wonder how they make a living.
You burn them with matches which you'd do
to no other creature, only this one. They have
never harmed you, but you prosecute based on
intent. Perhaps they only crave a little warmth,
but you see them, oiled and impossibly flat, and
you assume you know. You assure the dog that
you know.

Horses

She walks up the stream to where it emerges from the sandstone cliff,
    bends down to peer into the crease, narrow as the space between
    reeds of an oboe, slips through into the lung of a cave. Angled
    walls smell moss, smell water skirting stones like distant chimes. A
    scraping noise—animals pawing. Horses.
Dozens up to their fetlocks in water, shifting, slow tectonics.
She wants to yell, "Run, get out!" There is no
out. She chants against the cold.
Horses sing back, guttural undertones. The water rises.
They swim like a temple down the passage. Horses crushing white bones
    on salted walls down a cataract. Legs flail.
As they hit the emerald basin, the horses vaporize.
She grasps for a thin sliver of rock, watching their dark spiritual rain
vanish before her eyes: sisters, brothers, lost poems, children she never
    had.

JANE EASTWOOD

Contemplating the Future

We sit at the kitchen table, a difficult day. Your patient who survived
horrible cancer is itching again.

You cry. I wonder how someone with a heart tender as yours can
listen to people's sad ends. Those pitiable

moments when you hug them the last time and cry.
I take your hand grateful we're alive.

Sometimes you're fearful for when one of us will die. I dither on,
        unafraid.
My future: Blue sky glimpsed through arms of a full-grown oak. Your
        vision:

Sandy baseball lot when you were eight and the world
secure. I can't love you backward, so look ahead.

You look backward to those moments of good. It
keeps us in different futures. I keep holding your hand.

Misericord

For me it's enough, the early
light on a young maple bending forward against

arterial tangle of oak.
Deep in the background, some old spruce.

Take the Canadian shield, lay it over the
backcountry of your brain.

Pebbles that rush from wave's catch,
a few ten-thousand-year-old fish caught in stone.

Startle of scarlet shelf fungus
leaping from forest dark.

In the slippery descent of the boat into the lake,
to hear the water's green voice call

as you fall toward it and love the
thought of slipping under.

REBECCA WEAVER

Burn Scene

When after the door
and the glittering guards
and the light on the drive
you get up to the bar

the first burn of the night
the burn for the dancing
and the loose world anthropomorphizing
around you into legs come here through dark afternoons

then another burn
the burn of the voices of the singers
on the speakers and the speakers
screaming over the storm of the place the whole place

with its history of backdoors
and backdoors and underground tunnels
and the stubborn smell of the bouncers

and the dashing men who'll buy drinks
the dashing deep men
with their hair and their necklaces

and you're in there
after the shots and the cruising
all the way in there
without anything blurred
like you think it should be
with everybody you want
you want everybody
in there
all the way in there.

Gay Panic

Small triangles are never shields.
We must remember that.

That and that
blame rests nowhere
but in one's grip.

He will plead for his life,
they will plead for their lives,
we will plead for our lives.

Gay panic whips
the words
from his mouth:

with their arms striking out for distance
they won't hear him.
They stick the air full:

Law, memorial,
        law, memorial,
                law, memorial.

Pins through ribbons.

REBECCA WEAVER

Half-open now

for Cheleen Mahar

"open relationship" meant open on her side. This such on her cheekbone, this place of her primacy to you as a woman and the leftover half of the week she's with her.

So you do not know whether to promise return of the gift, the certainty of uncertainty in your reach—how what the two of you do can get you jailed there—

half-open now. Door open, but then her gloves and books. Of course the cats. *complicated, complicated*. Low-slung Nebraska motel and humidity now:

not think but lick off that place in your neck where the bone-ridge drops under skin on its way to head, slip fingers where Levi's drop below shirt and hips raise themselves delicate shelves,

swagger-slain laughter. You just said something funny but also alarming. Your laughter's surprised, too.

The sky above the church, the windows

Light from one source isn't always enough, I thought as you told me about the day you went out walking looking wandering around and you wandered into the church because something about the light around it struck you, something about what it didn't ask of you, so in your sweats you went in and told the secretary you had to talk to someone right now, standing there in your tennis shoes and wrist bands. Through a side door a woman said "talk to me" and you did. And now you're done with that, after talking to the minister, done with all that guilt you grew up with— what is a church anyway, you're saying now, but the people holding it, the light & the wandering—

CONTRIBUTORS

CRYSTAL BOSON is a queer poet living in Lawrence, KS, as a transplant from Texas. Her current collection of poetry is looking back across the Kansas landscape to the place she used to call home, and situating it within her current geographic and religious setting. She is currently a graduate student in American Studies at the University of Kansas. She lives next to a farm with her partner, their cat Delphina Jenkins Boson III, and her basil plant.

JES BRAUN, 28, likes writing, bikes, tea, running around outdoors and creating new clothes out of old crappy floppy clothes. She currently lives in Minneapolis and is pursuing a degree in debt and sciencey things from the University of Minnesota.

NATALIE J. BYERS lives in Joplin, MO. She graduated from Missouri Southern State University with a Bachelor degree in English with a double emphasis in Creative Writing and Professional/Technical Writing in May 2011. In the fall, she will attend Missouri State University in Springfield for her MA in Creative Writing. Though she spent her childhood in the deep South, she has lived in Missouri since she was eight years old and loves it here!

CHING-IN CHEN is the author of *The Heart's Traffic* (Arktoi Books/Red Hen Press). The daughter of Chinese immigrants, she is a Kundiman and Lambda Fellow and a member of the Voices of Our Nations Arts Foundation and Macondo writing communities. A community organizer, she has worked in the Asian American communities of San Francisco, Oakland, Riverside and Boston. Ching-In is a co-editor of *The Revolution Starts at Home: Confronting Intimate Violence Within Activist Communities* (South End Press). In Milwaukee, she is *Cream City Review's* editor-in-chief and involved in her union and the radical marching band, Milwaukee Molotov Marchers. [chinginchen.com]

CARLA CHRISTOPHER is a queer femme of color who currently lives in Pennsylvania after spending most of her life in Michigan. [facebook.com/poetrywarriorcarla]

JANE EASTWOOD lives and writes from her St. Paul home where she is continually enthralled by the changing sky out her study window. She has an MFA from Hamline University. Her work has been published in *ArtWord Quarterly, North Coast Review, The Evergreen Chronicles,* and *Sidewalks.*

JENNIFER-RIVER ELLER is a trans woman originally from Barnum, Minnesota and a graduate of Mankato State University's Creative Writing MFA program. She spends nine months of the year teaching British Literature in Prince George's County, Maryland and returns to Minnesota in the summers to work on short stories, poems, and novels. [caitlinsong.wordpress.com]

JESSICA VERSE GABRIELLE was born on the south side of Chicago, Illinois. While in Minnesota, Verse teamed up with a fellow artist and formed the spoken word duo Poetic Assassins, produced, wrote, and starred in the play *Eliminating Oppression One Ink Shell at a Time*, and formed the spoken word organization *Sai Werd Ink*. Coming from the Hip Hop tradition of community and consciousness mixed with complex rhymes and thought provoking lyrics, her work deals with issues such as class, race, gender, and identity. Verse has traveled the country promoting a collaborative album *Red D.O.T.T. (Death of the Truth)*, performing, leading workshops, and lecturing on issues of social justice and equality.

JULIE GARD lives in Duluth, Minnesota with her partner of twelve years, the poet Michelle Matthees, and their daughter, whom they met in Vladivostok, Russia. Originally from Philadelphia, she has lived in the Midwest for over 20 years, in Iowa, North Dakota, and Minnesota. She is an Assistant Professor of Writing at the University of Wisconsin-Superior and has published two chapbooks of prose poetry: *Russia in 17 Objects* (Tiger's Eye Press, 2011) and *Obscura: The Daguerreotype Series* (Finishing Line Press, 2007). Her poetry and short fiction has appeared in *The Prose Poem Project, Clackamas Literary Review, Crab Orchard Review, The MacGuffin*, and *Fiction Attic*. Awards include a Fulbright Graduate Fellowship and grants from the Barbara Deming Memorial Fund and the Arrowhead Regional Arts Council. [juliegard.com]

KATE LYNN HIBBARD's books of poems include *Sleeping Upside Down* (Silverfish Press, 2006) and *Sweet Weight* (Tiger Bark Press 2012). She is currently working on a manuscript of historical poetry about women's experiences in the Great Plains frontier. A professor of writing and women's studies at Minneapolis Community and Technical College, she lives with two cats, three dogs, and her partner Jan in Saint Paul. [hibbarka.wordpress.com]

ANDREA JENKINS is an award-winning poet and writer. Most recently she was awarded a Bush Fellowship and a Fellowship in the Cultural Community Leadership Institute at Intermedia Arts sponsored by the Bush Foundation, and named a fellow in the Many Voices Fellowship at the Playwrights' Center. Last year she won the Verve Grant for Spoken Artist at Intermedia Arts and the Naked Stages Grant for Emerging Performance Artist at Pillsbury House Theatre. She is a Givens Foundation Fellow working with Amiri Baraka and J. Otis Powell! She has won the Loft Mentor Series in 2002 and the Napa Valley Writers Conference scholarship in 2003. Andrea has an MFA in Creative Writing from Hamline University. [andreajenkins.webs.com]

C. BETH LOOFE, a gray-haired dyke originally from Davey, Nebraska, is an activist, a poet, a spoken word artist and the playful bane of her wife's existence. She has always been a small town girl—a Nebraska Woman—always able to speak her mind. A dangerous combination for an out lesbian armed with a pen.

SHEILA PACKA lives in Duluth, Minnesota and has lived in northern Minnesota all of her life. She has three books of poems, *The Mother Tongue, Echo & Lightning* and *Cloud*

CONTRIBUTORS

Birds, and edited an anthology of northern poets called *Migrations: Poetry and Prose for Life's Transitions*. Her work appears in *Good Poems, American Places*, edited by Garrison Keillor, and *To Sing Along the Way: Minnesota Women Poets from Pre-Territorial Times to the Present* edited by Joyce Sutphen, Thom Tammaro and Connie Wanek, as well as other anthologies. She has been Duluth Poet Laureate for 2010-2012. [sheilapacka.com]

CHRISTINE STARK is an award-winning writer and visual artist. Her fiction, poetry, and nonfiction have been published in numerous periodicals, anthologies, and academic journals. Her poem, "Momma's Song," was recorded by Fred Ho and the Afro Asian Ensemble and released as a double CD/manga titled *Deadly She-Wolf Assassin at Armageddon and Momma's Song*. Her novel, *Nickels: A Tale of Dissociation*, was a Lambda Literary Finalist. Christine's writing awards include a Pushcart Prize nomination, a McKnight Award, and a Loft Mentor Series in creative nonfiction, along with others. She teaches writing at Metropolitan State University in the Twin Cities and she lives in Minneapolis with her partner, April. [christinestark.com]

REBECCA WEAVER received her PhD from the University of Minnesota and her MFA from Hamline University and is a scholar, poet, teacher, and literary activist in the Twin Cities area. Her current poetry concerns the installation of light-rail and she is completing a manuscript based on her dissertation, entitled *The Urgency of Community: Poetry and the Counterculture in the 1970s*.

VALERIE WETLAUFER was born and raised in Iowa. She is currently a doctoral fellow in poetry at the University of Utah, but hopes to return to the Midwest upon graduation. She is Poetry Editor of *Quarterly West*. [valeriewetlaufer.com]

MORGAN GRAYCE WILLOW has published the poetry collections and chapbooks *Between, Silk*, and *The Maps are Words*. An award-winner in both poetry and prose, Morgan has received awards from the Minnesota State Arts Board, the McKnight Foundation, and The Witter Bynner Foundation. Her prose publications include "Class Struggles" in *Queerly Classed* (South End Press), and "Riding Shotgun for Stanley Home Products" in *Riding Shotgun: Women Write about their Mothers* (Borealis Books). Her poems have appeared in queer publications such as *Evergreen Chronicle, Equal Time, Sinister Wisdom, Malachite & Agate*, and the anthology *From Wedded Wife to Lesbian Life*. Morgan lives in Minneapolis with her partner of 22 years. [morgangraycewillow.com]

LAURA MADELINE WISEMAN has a doctorate from the University of Nebraska-Lincoln where she teaches English. She is the author of several chapbooks including *Branding Girls* (Finishing Line Press, 2011) and *She who Loves Her Father* (Dancing Girl Press, 2012). Her work has appeared in *Margie, Feminist Studies, Poet Lore, Cream City Review, Arts & Letters, Blackbird, American Short Fiction, 13th Moon, Prairie Schooner, Valparaiso Poetry Review*, and elsewhere. [lauramadelinewiseman.com]

WHEN WE BECOME WEAVERS

www.ingramcontent.com/pod-product-compliance
Lightning Source LLC
LaVergne TN
LVHW091201080426
835509LV00006B/770